Dear Parent:
Your child's love of reading starts here!

Every child learns to read in a different way and at his or her own speed. Some go back and forth between reading levels and read favorite books again and again. Others read through each level in order. You can help your young reader improve and become more confident by encouraging his or her own interests and abilities. From books your child reads with you to the first books he or she reads alone, there are I Can Read Books for every stage of reading:

SHARED READING
Basic language, word repetition, and whimsical illustrations, ideal for sharing with your emergent reader

BEGINNING READING
Short sentences, familiar words, and simple concepts for children eager to read on their own

READING WITH HELP
Engaging stories, longer sentences, and language play for developing readers

READING ALONE
Complex plots, challenging vocabulary, and high-interest topics for the independent reader

ADVANCED READING
Short paragraphs, chapters, and exciting themes for the perfect bridge to chapter books

I Can Read Books have introduced children to the joy of reading since 1957. Featuring award-winning authors and illustrators and a fabulous cast of beloved characters, I Can Read Books set the standard for beginning readers.

A lifetime of discovery begins with the magical words **"I Can Read!"**

*Visit www.icanread.com for information
on enriching your child's reading experience.*

*For Jennifer Rusin and all the students at Homestead
Elementary in Aurora, Illinois. —S.M.*

The author would like to thank the following people for sharing their
enthusiasm and expertise: Dr. John Lewis, director, Wildlife Vets
International; Dr. Craig Packer, director, Lion Center, University of
Minnesota; David Mizejewski, naturalist, the National Wildlife Federation;
and Dr. Kathy Quigley, international veterinary medicine.

The National Wildlife Federation and Ranger Rick contributors: Children's
Publication and Licensing Staff

I Can Read Book® is a trademark of HarperCollins Publishers.

Library of Congress Control Number: 2016949917
ISBN 978-0-06-243205-6 (trade bdg.) — ISBN 978-0-06-243206-3 (pbk.)

Typography by Brenda E. Angelilli

17 18 19 20 21 SCP 10 9 8 7 6 5 4 3 2 1 ❖ First Edition

Ranger Rick

I Wish I Was a Lion

by Sandra Markle

HARPER

An Imprint of HarperCollins Publishers

What if you wished you were a lion?

Then you became a lion.

Could you eat like a lion?

Sleep like a lion?

Live in a lion family?

And would you even want to?

Find out!

Where would you live?

Most lions live in Africa
in a grassy area called a savanna.
It's hot and dry here,
except in the rainy season.

Would you like to live outdoors?

Lions have a home range.
That's a place where they can find
food, water, and shade.

What would your family be like?

Lions live in a group called a pride.

There is at least one father lion.

Males are the biggest lions.

Only males have manes.

They guard the pride's home range.

There is also at least one

mother lioness.

Lionesses catch most of the food.

A lioness usually has
three or four babies called cubs.
She hides them until they can walk.
Then mother and cubs join the pride.

When the lionesses go hunting,
the cubs stay together.
They also play together.

What could be fun
about being in a pride?

What would you say in lion?

How would you talk?

Lions growl to say, "Leave me alone."

They hum to say, "I'm happy."

Only adults can ROAR to say,

"Stay away from my home range!"

Lions talk with their bodies, too.

A head bump says, "Hello."

A nuzzle says, "Glad we're together."

How would you learn to be a lion?

Cubs learn by playing.

They learn to hunt with a game
of sneaking up close and pouncing.

Cubs sometimes gang up to attack.

As adults, they'll use teamwork
to catch animals to eat.

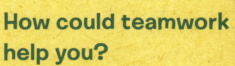

How could teamwork help you?

Cubs use their senses to learn.

They can see well—

both in sunlight and moonlight.

Cubs can hear faraway sounds. They use their long whiskers to feel things that are close.

When could long whiskers help you?

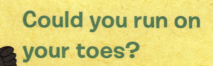

Could you run on
your toes?

Cubs also learn by exploring.
Everywhere they go,
lions walk and run on their toes.
Cubs learn that other animals,
such as elephants, share their home.

What would you eat?

Lions eat meat.

Lionesses catch the food.

Males guard the pride.

When the pride is together,

males always eat first.

If you ate like a lion, what food would you miss?

How would you wash up?

Lions lick their furry bodies clean.
Their rough tongues are perfect
for scraping off dirt and food.
Lions also groom one another,
because a lion can't lick
its own head.

Where would you sleep?

Lions sleep on the shady ground.

They sleep in trees when they can.

Being high makes sure

elephants won't wake them.

Lions sleep up to twenty hours a day.

They usually travel and hunt at night

when it's easier to sneak up

on other animals.

Would you like to sleep in a tree?

How would growing up change you?

At five months, a cub's spots fade.

By ten months, a cub is big enough
to hunt small animals.

A young male also grows his mane.

At two years old, lions are adults.

Then they can ROAR!

Being a lion could be cool for a while.

But do you want to sleep

twenty hours a day?

Lick yourself clean? Eat only meat?

And live outdoors in a pride?

Luckily, you don't have to.

You're not a lion.

You're YOU!

Did You Know?

🐾 A lion's roar can be heard for five miles (eight kilometers).

🐾 Adult lions can run as fast as 50 miles per hour (80 kilometers per hour). But only for short bursts.

🐾 Scientists found that lionesses choose males with dark manes. Usually only old, healthy males have dark manes.

🐾 Each lion's whiskers grow through a spot of dark fur. Like fingerprints, this spot pattern is different for each lion.

Fun Zone

Lions can react super-fast. That lets them catch speedy prey, such as antelope.

How quick can you react? Find out.

Have a partner hold a ruler with the zero-end down.

Now grab that ruler and hold it so your thumb is close to the zero.

Open your grip so your fingers no longer touch the ruler.

Get ready!

Have your partner decide when to let go.

Grab the falling ruler fast.

Next see which number is under your thumb.

The lower the number, the faster you were able to react.

Repeat two more times.

Do you get faster with practice? Lion cubs play sneak up close and pounce. That's how they get ready to hunt fast prey.

Wild Words

Cub: a young lion from birth to about 18 months old

Home range: the area within which an animal usually lives

Lion: a big cat that lives in prides; a male lion

Lioness: a female lion

Pride: a group of lions that lives and hunts together

Roar: the loud noise made by adult lions

Savanna: a grassy area of land with few trees

Dig Deeper
WANT TO FIND OUT EVEN MORE ABOUT LIONS?
Check out the Ranger Rick website: www.RangerRick.com
SEARCH: lions

Photography from the archives of the National Wildlife Federation—Floyd Brown, Christine Becker, Jacqueline Orsulak, Bob Miller, Randall Ward, Frederick Small, Theodore Mattas, Donald Bruschera, John Hobbs, Andrei Duman, Torrey Trust, and Greg Harvey (www.harveywildlifephotography.ca). The following photographs are © Getty Images: Front cover Photographer WLDavies; page 19 Photographer John Carnemolla